Sandhill
Cranes

written and photographed
by Lynn M. Stone

Lerner Publications Company • Minneapolis, Minnesota

For Charlotte and Mel, my parents, who lovingly cultivated and indulged my love of the world outdoors.

—LMS

Photographs in this book were taken at the International Crane Foundation, Baraboo, Wisconsin; Myakka River State Park, Florida; Hillsborough County, Florida; Sarasota County, Florida; McConnell River Migratory Bird Refuge, Northwest Territories, Canada; and Denali National Park, Alaska.

Additional photographs are reproduced with permission from: pp. 8–9, © D. Robert Franz/The Wildlife Collection; p. 17, © Ron Spomer; p. 25, © Henry H. Holdsworth/The Wildlife Collection; p. 42, © Tim Crosby/The Wildlife Collection.

Thanks to our series consultant, Sharyn Fenwick, elementary science/math specialist. Mrs. Fenwick was the winner of the National Science Teachers Association 1991 Distinguished Teaching Award. She also was the recipient of the Presidential Award for Excellence in Math and Science Teaching, representing the state of Minnesota at the elementary level in 1992.

Early Bird Nature Books were conceptualized by Ruth Berman and designed by Steve Foley. Series editor is Joelle Goldman.

Library of Congress Cataloging-in-Publication Data

Stone, Lynn M.
    Sandhill cranes / written and photographed by Lynn M. Stone.
       p. cm. – (Early bird nature books)
    Includes index.
    Summary: Describes the physical characteristics, habitat, behavior, and life cycle of one of the tallest birds in North America.
    ISBN 0-8225-3027-9
    1. Sandhill crane—Juvenile literature. [1. Sandhill crane. 2. Cranes (Birds)] I. Title. II. Series.
    QL696.G84S76 1997
    598.3'2—dc21   96-49981

Manufactured in the United States of America
1 2 3 4 5 6 – SP – 02 01 00 99 98 97

Contents

Alaska
(U.S.)

CANADA

UNITED
STATES

MEXICO

Sandhill cranes live in North America and Russia. The red areas show where sandhills can be found in North America.

Be a Word Detective

Can you find these words as you read about the sandhill crane? Be a detective and try to figure out what they mean. You can turn to the glossary on page 46 for help.

court

down feathers

flight feathers

flocks

habitats

incubates

migration

omnivores

predators

refuge

tundra

wetlands

Chapter 1

Sandhill cranes have lived in North America for millions of years. How tall is a sandhill crane?

A Long, Tall Bird

Hidden in the grass, the small snake is hard to see. But a bird with sharp eyes can see it. The bird runs toward the snake. Then the bird darts its head down. It jabs the snake with its beak. The sandhill crane has found a meal.

Sandhill cranes are tall birds. They are among the tallest birds in North America. When a sandhill crane is an adult, it is about as tall as you are. Its long legs and long neck make it tall.

Sandhill cranes have gray feathers. On the tops of their heads, they have a patch of bare, red skin. The skin looks like a red cap.

The patch of red on a sandhill's head is red skin.
Adult sandhills can be 4 to 5 feet tall.

Sandhill cranes make beautiful, musical sounds. They live in flocks for most of the year.

A sandhill crane has a voice like no other bird. Its call sounds like a bugle. The bugle sound is so loud that it can be heard 3 miles away. That is a long way. You might need more than an hour to walk 3 miles.

Most of the year, sandhill cranes live in groups called flocks. A hundred sandhills may live in one flock. Sometimes several flocks live near each other. When many birds call at the same time, the sound is very loud!

*Adult sandhills are gray, but young sandhills are brown.
Youngsters do not have a patch of red on their heads.*

Sandhills are just one species, or kind, of crane. There are 15 species of cranes in all. Whooping cranes are another species of crane. Sandhill cranes and whooping cranes are the only cranes who live in North America. Like sandhills, whooping cranes have red caps. But whooping cranes are not gray. They are white.

This white bird is a whooping crane. Very few whooping cranes are left in the world.

Chapter 2

A marsh is a good place to find sandhill cranes. In what other kinds of places can sandhills be found?

Sandhill Country

 The kinds of places where an animal can live are called its habitats. Sandhill cranes can live in several habitats.

Sandhills are often found in wetland habitats. Wetlands are muddy places with shallow water. A marsh is a kind of wetland.

Wetlands where sandhills live are often near meadows or fields. Sandhills hunt for food in wetlands. But on most days, sandhills also go to meadows or fields to hunt.

These sandhill cranes are hunting in a meadow.

Thousands of sandhill cranes spend the summer months on the tundra. The tundra is a large, treeless area in the far north. In the summer, the tundra is like a giant meadow with many lakes.

In summer, the tundra has many lakes. In winter, the tundra is covered with snow.

These sandhill cranes are flying over mountains in Alaska.

Almost all sandhills live in northern habitats during the warm months of the year. In these places, snow covers the ground in winter. Snow makes it hard for sandhills to find food. They leave before winter comes. They fly south to winter homes where there is no snow.

Cranes fly with their necks straight out, like spears. A sandhill's wings may spread 7 feet from tip to tip.

Sandhills fly north again in spring. They return to their summer homes. The trip between a bird's winter home and its summer home is called a migration.

Sandhills migrate together in large flocks. The birds can fly hundreds of miles in one day. They stop now and then to eat and to rest. They often stop in one place for several weeks.

Most sandhills fly south in the fall and north in the spring. Some fly 7,000 miles each year.

A flock of sandhills migrates to the same places each year. Most sandhills have summer homes in Canada, Alaska, and the northern states of the West and the Midwest. Their winter homes are in Florida, New Mexico, California, Texas, and Mexico.

This sandhill crane lives in Florida. Some sandhills stay in Florida all year.

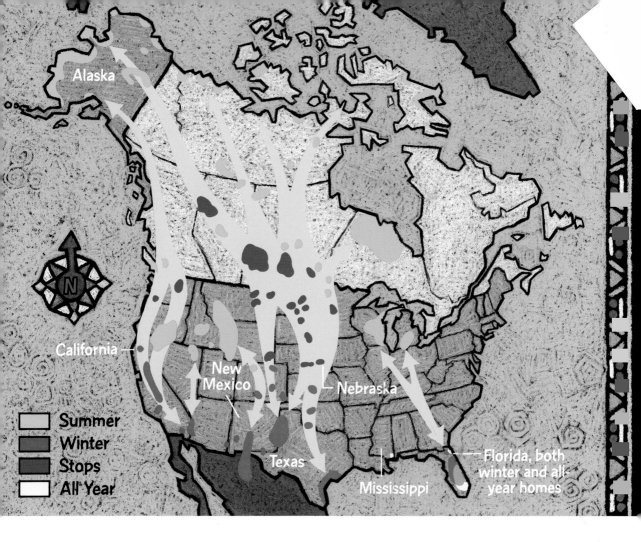

Summer
Winter
Stops
All Year

Alaska

California

New
Mexico

Nebraska

Texas

Mississippi

Florida, both
winter and all-
year homes

Migrating sandhills follow the paths shown on this map. The purple areas show where the birds stop to rest. Sandhills in the yellow areas stay there all year.

A few groups of sandhills do not migrate. They live all year long in Cuba, Mississippi, and Florida. In these places, snow never covers the ground. The cranes can always find food.

Chapter 3

A snake makes a good meal for a sandhill crane. What other kinds of food do sandhills eat?

Finding Food

Sandhill cranes are omnivores (OM-nuh-vorz). That means they eat both plants and animals. Sandhills eat mostly plants. They eat berries, roots, and seeds. They eat grains such as wheat, barley, and corn. They eat these grains in farm fields.

Sandhills also eat insects. They hunt small animals such as snakes, frogs, and mice. Sandhills jab with their sharp beaks to kill these animals. The birds are busy hunters. They keep moving. They walk and jab, walk and jab.

Sandhill cranes poke their beaks into the mud to find insects who live underground.

Sometimes sandhills hunt for food along a muddy shore. They eat crayfish and other animals who live in the mud. To get this food, sandhills poke their beaks into the mud.

Sometimes a sandhill wades into the water. It puts its head underwater. Then it pokes its beak into the muddy bottom.

A sandhill crane's long legs are good for wading in shallow water.

Sometimes sandhills reach high into tall plants to find insects.

When sandhills eat a small animal such as a mouse, they swallow it in one gulp. Sometimes a sandhill eats a larger animal such as a big salamander. The bird pecks this food into pieces. Then the bird eats it.

Chapter 4

Male and female sandhills look alike. What do a male and a female sandhill do when they court?

Starting a Family

During spring migration, sandhill cranes court. Courting is a way of choosing a partner. A male and a female court each other.

To court, sandhills make loud calls. They flap their wings. They leap into the air. They bow their heads. In this way, a male and a female get each other's attention. Then they form a pair.

When two sandhills court, they look as if they are dancing. After they court, they start a new family.

When a flock of sandhills reaches its summer home, the flock breaks up. Pairs go off on their own. Each pair chooses a place to build a nest, far from other sandhills.

Both the male and the female sandhill build the nest. They often build it on dry, sandy ground. Sometimes they build it in a marsh.

This sandhill crane nest is in a marsh in Florida. Sandhill mothers usually lay two eggs each year.

This sandhill nest is on the tundra in Canada.

Sandhills make their nests out of plants. In a marsh, they use cattail plants. Nests made of cattails look like big bushel baskets.

In dry places, sandhills build smaller nests. These nests may be made of a few leaves and bits of moss.

Sandhill crane parents take turns sitting on their eggs.

The mother sandhill lays one egg in the
nest. The baby inside the egg cannot get too
hot or too cold, or it will die. So the mother
incubates (ING-kyuh-bates) the egg by sitting on
it. Incubating keeps the egg at the right
temperature.

In a day or two, the mother lays one more egg. After that, the mother and the father sandhill take turns incubating the eggs.

This sandhill parent is leaving its nest to stretch and to eat. The bird will return to the nest soon.

This sandhill crane is pretending to be hurt. It wants to keep an enemy away from its nest. Enemies chase hurt birds because hurt birds make an easy meal. If the enemy follows the sandhill, it may not find the bird's nest.

This bobcat might eat a sandhill egg. Raccoons, foxes, crows, eagles, owls, and other enemies also eat sandhill eggs.

Sandhill parents keep other animals away from their nest. They attack any sandhills who come too near. The parents also attack predators (PRED-uh-turz). Predators are animals who hunt and eat other animals. Some predators, such as raccoons, eat sandhill eggs.

Chapter 5

This baby sandhill could stand in the palm of your hand. How long does a sandhill chick stay in its nest?

Growing Up

Sandhill parents incubate their eggs for about a month. Then their babies hatch. Baby sandhill cranes are called chicks. Chicks are covered with short, fluffy down feathers. Down feathers are soft and warm.

When chicks are a few hours old, their parents lead them away from the nest. The birds do not go back to the nest again.

Chicks can swim, but they cannot fly. That is because they do not have flight feathers. Flight feathers are the stiff feathers on a bird's wings and tail that help it fly.

Sandhill chicks can cheep and purr. They cannot make loud bugle sounds like their parents.

Chicks catch some of their own food. They run along the ground, snapping at insects. But it is hard to catch enough food this way. Mostly, chicks get food from their parents. The parents carry the food in their beaks. They may put the food right into a baby's mouth. Often they drop it in front of a chick.

Chicks learn how to hunt by watching their parents.

A sandhill parent brings food to its chick until the chick is almost full grown.

This sandhill youngster is jabbing its brother or sister with its beak.

The two chicks in a sandhill family often fight over food. The chick who hatched first is usually bigger than the other chick. The bigger chick takes most of the food. The smaller chick does not get as much to eat. Sometimes the bigger chick kills the smaller chick.

Chicks also face another danger. They cannot fly away from predators such as foxes, raccoons, and bobcats. Usually only one chick in a sandhill family lives to be an adult.

When a chick is eight or nine weeks old, it is almost as big as its parents.   It has flight feathers. It runs along and flaps its wings. It learns to fly.

Young sandhills grow fast. This youngster is stretching its wings.

A sandhill family stays together for almost a year. Then a young sandhill leaves its parents and joins other youngsters. The youngsters live in a flock together until they are ready to start families of their own.

Some sandhills start families when they are two years old. But sandhills may be as old as seven when they first start families.

Chapter 6

Sandhill cranes need lots of open land and water. Do most sandhills live near cities?

Sandhills and People

Most sandhill cranes live in wild places far from cities. Northern sandhills have many wild places in which to live. So do the sandhills in Florida.

A sandhill crane and its baby are hunting for food on this golf course.

In some places, sandhill habitat is disappearing. People have drained the water from wetlands. There is land where the water used to be. People have moved into these places. They have built cities, roads, and farms. Sandhills cannot live there anymore.

40

In Mississippi, there are few places left where sandhills can live. The sandhill cranes in Mississippi are endangered. Very few of them are left.

But people are helping the Mississippi sandhills. People have set aside a safe place for them. This safe place is called a refuge (REF-yooj).

These scientists are studying a sandhill crane nest. They are being careful not to hurt the eggs.

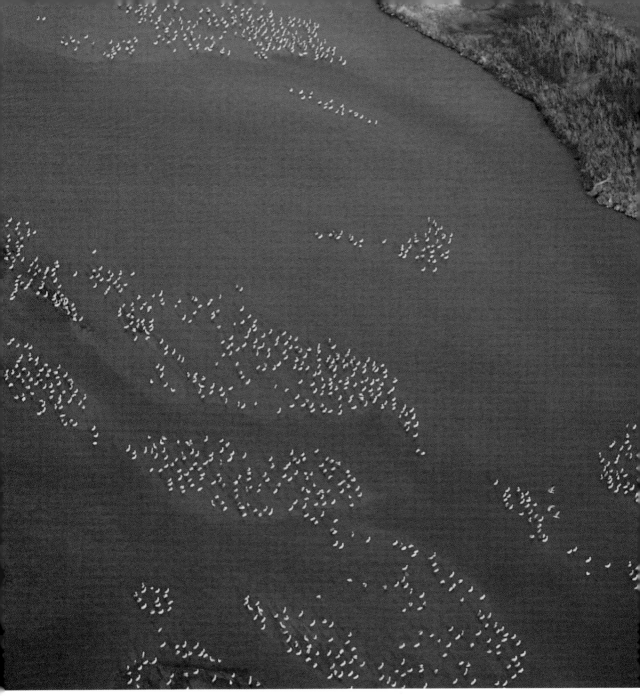

Every year, migrating sandhills stop at the Platte River. The birds rest and eat for a few weeks. In this picture, the birds look like white dots.

Sandhill cranes have survived for millions of years.

Another safe place for sandhills is in Nebraska. It is along the Platte River. People have set aside many places for sandhills. By saving these places, people help save these birds and their beautiful, wild music.

On Sharing a Book

As you know, adults greatly influence a child's attitude toward reading. When a child sees you read, or when you share a book with a child, you're sending a message that reading is important. Show the child that reading a book together is important to you. Find a comfortable, quiet place. Turn off the television and limit other distractions, such as telephone calls.

   Be prepared to start slowly. Take turns reading parts of this book. Stop and talk about what you're reading. Talk about the photographs. You may find that much of the shared time is spent discussing just a few pages. This discussion time is valuable for both of you, so don't move through the book too quickly. If the child begins to lose interest, stop reading. Continue sharing the book at another time. When you do pick up the book again, be sure to revisit the parts you have already read. Most importantly, enjoy the book!

Be a Vocabulary Detective
You will find a word list on page 5. Words selected for this list are important to the understanding of the topic of this book. Encourage the child to be a word detective and search for the words as you read the book together. Talk about what the words mean and how they are used in the sentence. Do any of these words have more than one meaning? You will find these words defined in a glossary on page 46.

What about Questions?
Use questions to make sure the child understands the information in this book. Here are some suggestions:

   What did this paragraph tell us? What does this picture show? What do you think we'll learn about next? Could a sandhill crane live in your backyard? Why/Why not? Why do most sandhill cranes leave their summer homes each fall? Why do some sandhill cranes stay in one place all year? What do sandhill cranes eat? How is a sandhill crane family like your family, and how is it different? What do you think it's like being a sandhill crane? What is your favorite part of the book? Why?

If the child has questions, don't hesitate to respond with questions of your own, such as: What do *you* think? Why? What is it that you don't know? If the child can't remember certain facts, turn to the index.

Introducing the Index

The index is an important learning tool. It helps readers get information quickly without searching throughout the whole book. Turn to the index on page 48. Choose an entry, such as *beaks,* and ask the child to use the index to find out how sandhill cranes use their beaks. Repeat this exercise with as many entries as you like. Ask the child to point out the differences between an index and a glossary. (The index helps readers find information quickly, while the glossary tells readers what words mean.)

Where in the World?

Many plants and animals found in the Early Bird Nature Books series live in parts of the world other than the United States. Encourage the child to find the places mentioned in this book on a world map or globe. Take time to talk about climate, terrain, and how you might live in such places.

All the World in Metric!

Although our monetary system is in metric units (based on multiples of 10), the United States is one of the few countries in the world that does not use the metric system of measurement. Here are some conversion activities you and the child can do using a calculator:

WHEN YOU KNOW:	MULTIPLY BY:	TO FIND:
miles	1.609	kilometers
feet	0.3048	meters
inches	2.54	centimeters
gallons	3.787	liters
tons	0.907	metric tons
pounds	0.454	kilograms

Activities

Make up a story about sandhill cranes. Be sure to include information from this book. Draw or paint pictures to illustrate your story.

Pretend you're a sandhill crane chick. What kinds of sounds do you make? How do you get food? How do you learn to fly?

Visit a zoo to see sandhill cranes, whooping cranes, and other cranes. What are the differences among the cranes? How are cranes similar to other birds, and how are they different?

Glossary

court—to attract a partner

down feathers—soft, fluffy feathers

flight feathers—long, stiff feathers that help a bird to fly

flocks—groups of animals of one kind who live together

habitats—the areas where a kind of animal can live and grow

incubates (ING-kyuh-bates)—sits on eggs to keep them the right temperature so they'll hatch

migration—the trip between an animal's summer home and its winter home

omnivores (OM-nuh-vorz)—animals who eat both plants and animals

predators (PRED-uh-turz)—animals who hunt other animals

refuge (REF-yooj)—a safe place

tundra—a place in the far north where the ground is frozen almost all year

wetlands—places with muddy soil

Index

Pages listed in **bold** type refer to photographs.